Jaden Smith

ABDO
Publishing Company

Big Buddy BOOKS
Buddy Bios

by Sarah Tieck

Coordinating Series Editor: Rochelle Baltzer
Contributing Editors: Megan M. Gunderson, BreAnn Rumsch, Marcia Zappa
Graphic Design: Maria Hosley
Cover Photograph: *Getty Images*: Carlos Alvarez.
Interior Photographs/Illustrations: *AP Photo*: Gregg DeGuire/MTV/PictureGroup via AP IMAGES (p. 21), Phelan M. Ebenhack/AP Images for Best Buy (p. 18), FILE (p. 21), Gaas (pp. 7, 13), Peter Kramer (p. 15), Israel Leal (p. 19), Chris Pizzello (p. 17), Matt Sayles (p. 25), Sipa via AP Images (p. 29), Berthold Stadler (p. 5); *Getty Images*: Avik Gilboa/WireImage (p. 9), Claire Greenway (p. 26), Jim Smeal/WireImage (p. 17), Ray Tamarra (p. 11), Paul Warner/WireImage (p. 23); *Shutterstock*: Mikhail Nekrasov (p. 25).

Library of Congress Cataloging-in-Publication Data

Tieck, Sarah, 1976-
  Jaden Smith : talented actor / Sarah Tieck.
    p. cm. -- (Big buddy biographies)
  ISBN 978-1-61714-707-4
  1. Smith, Jaden, 1998- Juvenile literature. 2. Motion picture actors and actresses--United States--Biography--Juvenile literature. I. Title.
  PN2287.S585T54 2011
  791.4302'8092--dc22
  [B]
                              2010034216

Contents

Rising Star

Jaden Smith is a young actor. He has appeared in popular movies. In 2010, Jaden starred in *The Karate Kid*. Jaden is also known for being part of a famous family.

In *The Karate Kid*, Jaden's character is named Dre Parker.

Family Ties

Jaden Christopher Syre Smith was born in Los Angeles, California, on July 8, 1998. His parents are Will Smith and Jada Pinkett Smith. Jaden has an older brother named Trey and a younger sister named Willow.

The Smiths often attend movie openings and other events together.

Did you know...

Jaden and Trey are very close. Trey is Jaden's half brother. He is Will's son from his first marriage.

Growing Up

Jaden grew up in the Los Angeles area. Both his parents are famous actors.

Will and Jada have acted on television and in movies. They have worked as **producers**, too. And, Will has made **rap** albums.

Jaden has learned about working
as an actor from his parents.

Jaden often travels with his parents for their work. So, he and his sister don't attend regular schools.

When they were young, Jaden and Willow worked with private teachers at home. Around 2005, they began learning with other homeschooled children. And in 2008, the Smiths started a private school. Both Jaden and Willow have attended this school.

Jaden says he enjoys learning math because he is good at it.

Starting Out

In 2006, Jaden acted in his first movie. He had an important **role** in *The Pursuit of Happyness*. The movie is based on a real-life story. It is about a man caring for his son after losing his home.

In *The Pursuit of Happyness*, Jaden worked with his dad. Jaden's character was the son of Will's character. Jaden learned a lot about acting and making movies from this role.

Jaden and Will worked with actress Thandie Newton in *The Pursuit of Happyness*. She played Jaden's mom in the movie.

13

A Working Actor

Jaden's first movie **role** helped people notice his talent. Then in 2008, Jaden acted in *The Day the Earth Stood Still*. He played an important role!

In this science fiction movie, an alien comes to Earth. Jaden plays a boy named Jacob. Will and Jada gave their son acting tips for the sad scenes.

Jaden worked with well-known actors Jennifer Connelly and Keanu Reeves in *The Day the Earth Stood Still.*

In the Spotlight

Jaden's brother and sister are famous, too! When Trey was young, Will wrote a **rap** song about him called "Just the Two of Us." Trey appeared with Will in the song's music video.

Soon after Jaden started acting, Willow followed. In 2007, she appeared in *I Am Legend* with her dad. And in 2008, Willow had a **role** in *Kit Kittredge: An American Girl*.

Will wrote a book about Trey. It was called *Just the Two of Us.*

Willow worked with Abigail Breslin in *Kit Kittredge.*

Even when they work with their parents, Jaden and Willow have to try out for roles.

Jaden did a rap in a song with Justin Bieber for *The Karate Kid*. The song is called "Never Say Never."

Big Break

In 2010, Jaden starred in the movie *The Karate Kid*. This was his first lead **role**!

In the movie, Jaden plays Dre Parker. Dre moves from the United States to China. When he is bullied, his friend Mr. Han teaches him **kung fu**.

Fans and reporters took pictures of Jaden at *The Karate Kid* openings around the world.

The Karate Kid is a remake of a 1984 film of the same name. Will had the idea to remake it. He and Jada were **producers** of the 2010 movie.

The Karate Kid was popular with fans. Reporters **interviewed** Jaden about his **role** in the movie. Stories and pictures of him appeared in magazines and newspapers.

The first Karate Kid movies are about a boy named Daniel. When Daniel moves to a new town, other kids bully him. So, he learns karate from Mr. Miyagi to protect himself.

In *The Karate Kid*, famous actor Jackie Chan played Mr. Han. Jackie is known for his skills in martial arts, such as kung fu.

An Actor's Life

Jaden attends events and meets excited fans. Will often goes with him.

As an actor, Jaden spends time practicing lines. During filming, he works on a movie set for several hours each day.

For certain roles, Jaden may have to learn new skills. For his part in *The Karate Kid*, Jaden spent several months learning kung fu!

Sometimes, Jaden travels to other states or countries to make movies. He may be away from home for a couple of months. He went to Beijing, China, to work on *The Karate Kid*. Some scenes were filmed on the Great Wall of China.

In *The Karate Kid*, Jaden and Jackie's characters train together along the Great Wall of China.

The Smiths attend events that raise money to help others.

Off the Screen

When Jaden is not working, he spends time at home. He enjoys hanging out with his family.

Helping other people is important to Jaden and his family. He and Willow work to help sick children in Africa. And, they do work in their own community.

Buzz

Jaden's fame continues to grow. He plans to continue working on movies. Fans are excited to see what's next for Jaden Smith. Many believe he has a bright **future**!

Jaden is comfortable in the spotlight.
He is used to fans taking his picture
and asking for autographs.

Snapshot

★**Name**: Jaden Christopher Syre Smith

★**Birthday**: July 8, 1998

★**Birthplace**: Los Angeles, California

★**Appearances**: *All of Us, The Pursuit of Happyness, The Day the Earth Stood Still, The Karate Kid*

Important Words

future (FYOO-chuhr) a time that has not yet occurred.

interview to ask someone a series of questions.

kung fu a Chinese fighting art, often practiced as a sport.

producer a person who oversees the making of a movie, a play, an album, or a radio or television show.

rap a type of music in which the words of a song are spoken to a beat.

role a part an actor plays.

set the place where a movie or a television show is recorded.

Web Sites

To learn more about Jaden Smith, visit ABDO Publishing Company online. Web sites about Jaden Smith are featured on our Book Links page. These links are routinely monitored and updated to provide the most current information available.

www.abdopublishing.com

Index